ABOUT THE AUTHOR

Gary has been writing poetry since the age of 16, when keeping a diary became too monotonous. All of his poetry, which is rhymed, is a reflection of what he has experienced or overheard or been exposed to.

Throughout his journey through life he has experienced important changes to popular culture and politics.
He grew up during the HIV epidemic and the Section 28 protests, then as a member of the military served through the two Gulf Wars, the Balkans conflict, the Northern Ireland peace process, Afghanistan, North Africa and the rise of the Islamic state, as well as working for the Prime Minister and the Royal family. These have all been key moments of experience for him.

Gary Niel Hitching

RUN THEY SAID...

Poetry of a Fortunate Airman

AUSTIN MACAULEY PUBLISHERS™

LONDON · CAMBRIDGE · NEW YORK · SHARJAH

A CIP catalogue record for this title is available from the
British Library.

ISBN 9781528916004 (Paperback)
ISBN 9781398401365 (ePub e-book)

www.austinmacauley.com

First Published 2021
Austin Macauley Publishers Ltd
1 Canada Square
Canary Wharf
London
E14 5LQ

DEDICATION

I have been inspired by my fortunate life in the Royal Air Force, without which I wouldn't have seen or experienced the amazing moments within my life. *Per Ardua Ad Astra.*

POEMS

How It All Started

I have never really been a writer,
More of a doer and an exciter.
Always had an active life,
Had a career, child and a wife.
Always hid my secrets well,
Pushing for the future, past not to dwell.
Changing in sexuality, change in career.
Always strong, not with any fear.
Well, that is always what I would like you to see,
Never to get inside the real me,
Opening my life, its paths and twists,
With its amazing chances of opportunities missed.
Inside this book lies the real me
And all the hurt pain and sorrow I see.
A life in poems, who would have thought,
The hatred, pain and sorrow I caught?
Come inside, pick it all apart,
For the conscience is the finest art...

Clean Me and Make Me a Man...

The day I found out I was really gay
I knew it was time to leave and run away;
Run away from proof and desires,
To start a life where nobody would guess my inner fires;
To run from trouble that could brew,
To start a life somewhere new,
To become a man and dampen down my thoughts,
And avoid the embarrassment of being caught;
To become the man that holds a gun
And no more hiding and having to run;
To prove to myself I'm normal, not weird,
And have a normal life, not one I feared.
The military will stop my will
And instead of lust I will learn to kill...

Concerned that the secret of my sexuality was about to be found out by my family and friends after a few private liaisons, I decided to sign up and join the Royal Air Force on a nine-year service contract. This would 'clean' me and turn me into a man, even if I was only 16!

However, the training proved to be even harder than I expected as I battled with the inner demons of my sexuality.

Morning Inspection

"Inspection – stand by your bed,"
The Angry handsome sergeant said.
I would have done everything he asked.
I found it hard to stand there wearing a mask,
A mask that covered my true inner feelings,
But if it was removed there would be rough dealings.
Hide it as much as I can,
Even in showers I hid, not much like a man,
Trying to force my demon away,
To talk and behave like a man not a girly gay.
Each day it got harder and harder than before
Hiding emotion under a manly, closed door,
Until I realised that I could not let it out;
I would now lose my job and my family without any doubt.
Although the family would forgive straightaway,
Nobody wants to be related to a gay.
So carry on learning about being a man,
Pushing weird feelings away as much as I can,
Turning all my thoughts into humour,
Whilst trying to kill this vile gay tumour.
Solace came when I finally finished training:
I was clearly a man now, although it had been draining.
Pushed my lurid thoughts to the back of my mind,
Concentrating on career and making sure that shined.
Onwards I go, denying myself the right:
My career as a man is now looking bright...

After completing all of my training, fighting with my inner self again, I graduated a man. For now my feelings have been dampened, ready to continue my life in the military – for the time being, anyway...

New Job, New Life

I'm here now, what do I do?
No parents to show me in my life that's new.
A room, a radio and a bed:
That's all I have now, no thoughts in my head.
A teenager in a man's world, earning my keep,
Not following others like a lost old sheep.
A new job, new friends, new life for me,
No memories or carnal thoughts to haunt me,
It's lonely being a teenager in a man's world,
Another one of life's balls slightly curled.
Loneliness can eat a young man's heart,
Breeds all kinds of thoughts and tears you apart.
In the back of my mind the demons still remain,
However now I'm in control and they are tame.
Time to move and grow up, do something with my life,
Build myself into a better man and find a wife,
Do normal things that families take part in:
Perhaps it's time to be somebody else's next of kin.

At 19 years old, I was ready to move to my new next job within
the Air Force. I decided I would find a wife and settle down,
putting my demons about my sexuality to bed forever, or so I
hoped...

Time to Become the Man

A new job, new town, new friends, a few years older;
Nothing really has changed, a moustache and now
  I'm bolder
On my mind all the time is settling down,
A wife and baby will be my crown.
Hard to find one whilst battling with thoughts.
When my eyes and heart a lady I caught,
We dated a while and moved in,
Lived a strange life deciding if we should be next of kin.
Realising the relationship suited us both,
It was decided quickly to betroth:
Not six months did pass from meeting to wed.
My only concern was the marital bed,
Pushing my demons away and to the back of mind,
Adjusting myself to be considerate and kind,
Not to be selfish and cruel and vicious,
Being wary that I wasn't being surreptitious.
Shortly after the wedding I was drafted overseas for
  a while.
To the Falkland Islands I left with a smile,
Realising I had achieved my quest:
I'm now a husband so nobody could contest.
Prior to leaving I received amazing news from my wife:
In our short time together she was carrying new life...

---

*I was on my way to the Falkland Islands having achieved
"normality", although the things I would see down there would
change my poetry to include more raw emotions and pity. I
would also still continue to battle not only with my sexuality
but with guilt.*

More Graves than Houses

Crosses and poppies everywhere:
Like all wars they are not fair.
Young men die in the prime of life,
Leaving at home children and a wife,
To remain in a cold lonely desolate land,
Only touched by an aggressive hand;
Harsh weather, storms and a constant gale,
Leaving behind reminders of the people who fail,
An abandoned toothbrush and a lonesome shoe,
An old burnt piece of land and a rusty old screw.
Not much remains of the three-month war,
Just memories and people enjoying a battlefield tour.
Laughter and regrowth are all on the way
Back of their minds they fear the day
When war will happen once again,
And lives will be torn to pieces with the destruction
  of men.

After a few weeks of settling down on the Falkland Islands at RAF Mount Pleasant, I was able to take a trip out to Tumbledown mountain where there was a large battle for Port Stanley between Argentinian and British troops. As there is minimal tourism on the islands a lot of personal and military equipment remains, showing me my first look at the cold light of war. Little did I know that I would see a lot more in the future and unfortunately a lot worse.

Mines

Danger mines, the sign said:
Enter here and you should surely be dead.
There are sheep roaming around everywhere,
Walking around the mines, not treading with care.
Bang and now wool flies everywhere,
The sheep should have taken more care.
The legacy of these devilish things
And all the destruction that they bring
Will linger for years and years to come
And will rear their heads and strike you dumb.
A coward's way of warfare' not playing by the rules,
These things can't even be removed with the most
  advanced tools.
Still dangerous today,
In the ground these metal scorpions stay.
Maybe they will stop future war
Allowing people to see the damage from before,
But for now they they remain volatile and clever,
Sitting in the ground forever and ever.

Whilst on another outing from Mount Pleasant to take photo-graphs of the minefields I saw an unfortunate sheep get blown up. The image of this remains with me to this day.

Load Up the Trolley, Boys

Bread, butter and tins of meat,
Honey, jam and glucose sweets:
Not a picnic for a fun day out
But a survival pack for people living in doubt.
Twelve hours a day running food supplies;
At night time, though, aid turns to lies.
After dark it's guns and ammunition,
For people keeping families alive is their mission.
During the dawn the city awakes,
And war continues and the ground shakes.
A day will come when the picnic is for fun,
And man, the man will have a football instead of a gun.
Until that day keep your eyes wide open,
Keep the city alive and the people hoping.
Keeps life's wheels turning,
Ignoring cars and people burning,
Through strength and determination
Blooms a strong and happy nation.
In the future peacetime will come
And their children will enjoy picnic fun,
Until then, boys, fill that trolley,
Forget al their melancholy.
Bar is open tonight, you can have one beer:
Drinking that will control your fear.

I was deployed to Sarajevo during the Balkans war, working at Sarajevo airport for the UN. We had a tunnel which had tracks to the city of Sarajevo: during the day it was my job to load up the trolley and ensure it was dispatched and pulled through with ropes by the people who were under siege. The UN fed that city for five years; I did it for four months.

Birth of a Child

The amazing feeling when you got everything right,
And probably the best ever birthday night:
A small person who has my eyes and smile
Looks back at me and considers a while.
I look back at her with pride and pleasure,
Knowing that this small package for life I will treasure.
No matter how difficult things ever become,
This little person will have a loving dad and mum.
Amazed that this has happened to me,
And now my demons must be gone; surely I'm free.

---

*I still look back on this night as one of the highlights of my life.
I didn't realise then that my time with my daughter wouldn't be
that long, unfortunately.*

Northern Ireland

"Check under your car for booby traps,"
Is what the briefing said, to avoid mishaps.
Sign out of the base and keep an eye out
As the terrorist doesn't care when he's about.
Bomb-damaged stock in the shops in Belfast,
A dangerous way of living; everyday there's a blast.
Another man killed in the street
As the guidelines to religion he didn't meet.
Pavements painted in tribal colours
To warn people it's dangerous for others.
More fighting again on the streets
Riots as well after an Orange meet.
The water cannons get deployed
Sprayed onto suited men, very annoyed.
It's the 12th day of July, a festival to celebrate the
   Orange guys.
This celebration is always filled with fear and dread
As a number of boys, military and civilian, will end
   up dead.
The terrorists appear to work on both sides,
Killing causing pain and with the devil they ride.
A peace process is to be happening soon
When all men will meet and play the same tune.
However, until that day men continue to fight
And phosphorus and fire light up the night.
Not a nice place for a family to live
Even if both sides sit down, talk and forgive.

---

*I moved to Northern Ireland with the "new family" and soon
realised that it was no place to bring a family up, so they
returned to England and I visited once a month. Unfortunately
for me, when they left my demons returned...*

Crash and a Bang

Men in the bar laughing and drinking
Made me stop and start thinking:
How long are we to be on this earth?
And when we are here what would be our worth?
The men I saw laughing were not here that long
For the next day they would all be gone
In fog they would all die in an unfortunate fire
When their aircraft crashed on the Mull of Kintyre.
I know these people have proved there worth
On their short-lived time on the harsh place called earth.

I worked in the Officers' Mess bar: the chaps who crashed their aircraft in fog the next day unfortunately all died. There have been investigations; however, everybody still has suspicions. Per Ardua Ad astra, my friends.

The Peace Process Begins

Whilst watching the news tonight,
Prior to the peace process there was a terrible fright"
A huge bomb in Omagh,
Hidden underneath a car.
The policeman moved people back
As they had been informed of the terrorist attack.
Unfortunately the location was wrong
And now the poor Spanish schoolchildren are all gone.
Terrorists must feel no pain
As when children die things aren't the same.
It certainly helped the peace process,
As everybody voted a very big yes.
So children didn't die in vain:
It taught a country that how they were living was insane.
The same ever as before:
Lots of people die to end future wars.

I saw the terrible news on the television and unfortunately within the next few days after this hosted the families of the murdered whilst they stayed on the base. A very sad time. However, peace still remains in Northern Ireland today; it's just a shame so many had to die for it to happen.

Not long after this happened, I moved back to England to start a new job as military cabin crew: a job that would send me round the world, seeing amazing and terrible sights.

Run They Said

They said run, so I did,
Ran fast with panic and fear and I hid.
Smoke, noise and fire everywhere,
People sat at home without a care.

They said run, don't hide,
So run I did, taking giant strides
Into a shelter, dark, damp and hot,
Thinking about my family and what I have got.

Run they said, so I did again.
It's lies when they say the sword isn't as mighty as
  the pen:
The sword hurts and cuts deep,
Making families cry and strong men weep.

Run they said, so I did once more,
Thinking, *Why is this happening, for who and what for?*

Run they said, but now I cannot:
The rain of fire came, large bangs and a shot.
I'm peaceful now the noise has gone;
My light is dull when previously it shone.

Run they said...

I wrote this on my first day in Basrah airport as it came under massive attack that night by insurgents.

Shooting Star

Sitting on a rickety barbed wire fence,
Smoking a cigarette in an atmosphere so very tense.
A beautiful clear moonlit sky:
No light pollution, you can see so high.
Stars so pretty and bright;
Nothing can ruin such an enchanting night.
A streak in the sky with a flaming tail,
A dying star's light as it begins to fail,
Keeps getting brighter but now it has noise...
Oh no, it's no star, it's a missile, boys!
Run, take cover, hide, don't fear,
Let out a gasp and shed a little tear.
Onto the ground now with a powerful bang:
The ground shakes, buildings quake, life balance hangs.
I long for the day the moon lights the sky,
When my only concern is the colour of my tie.
Until that day I will continue this career,
Preserving my life and fighting back my tear.

Written in Baghdad: I was sat on a fence smoking, talking to my mate. We were waiting for the next aircraft to come in as we would be swapping crews and going home. I wrote it in an air raid shelter whilst waiting for the all-clear.

Burning Light of Hope

Under a regime for years,
With strict rules, anger and tears,
A city which shone with fluorescent light
Now has an eerie glow lighting up the night:
Oil wells burning throughout the city,
Black smoke hiding all the pity.
Dreams are starting to get reborn
When previously lives were shattered and torn.
Destruction and anger always comes before
Blood's fighting and fields of gore,
When the fires begin to waiver
And there are no heroes or a saviour.
Life rebuilds and smoke dispels,
Food and perfume replace putrid smells.
But for now fire and smoke remain:
A new way of living and anger we should tame.
Fire will always burn on fuel,
Removing the core the heat will cool;
Black will become blue and red become green,
And the past will seem one big bad dream.

After the liberation of Baghdad, Saddam Hussein's army lit all the fire wells. They could be clearly seen from the outskirts of the city, where I wrote this.

You Know You're Dead

You know they're dead when the fields are red
And children don't cry anymore.

You know they're dead when the fields are red
And democracy knocks at your door.

You know they're dead when the fields are red
And nobody remembers the war.

You know they're dead when the fields are red
And money shakers are waiting on the floor.

You know they're dead when the fields are red
And life has no meaning anymore.

You know you're dead when the fields aren't red
And silence is the focus and the core.

You know you're dead when the fields aren't red
Nothing changes; it's the same as before...

This poem was written whilst I was on parade at the Cenotaph in London, for the 11th November Remembrance Day services attended by HM The Queen. I stood for two hours in the cold and rain, reciting this poem to stop myself passing out!

Smoky Stairs to Heaven

Upon walking into work I caught a glimpse of the news,
I was hurrying as I was part of the standby crews.
Watched an aircraft hit a tower abroad,
Wasn't paying much attention, as I recall;
Realised soon enough the world would change forever
And the fight of this silent war we will all endeavour.
Soon we were the only passenger aircraft flying
Whilst the twin towers collapsed and people were dying.
On our way to Washington, to drop off and collect,
Flying down the eastern seaboard able to pay my respects.
Approaching New York is normally an impressive sight:
Today, dark smoke blocks out sunlight.
The tower of smoke reaches up to space
With curves and twists with style and grace.
Was a sombre passing on the descent to Washington
Knowing that thousands of families are separated
  and gone.
Lonely aircraft in the American skies
Where fast jets buzzed around us like flies.
Landing cannot come quickly enough.
Flying through people's souls is tough,
But I'm sure it's part of life's big plan:
This event will move half of America to Afghanistan,
Where they will hunt and seek out evil,
An eye for an eye, these troops will kill.
A fire has lit in all Americans' hearts;
Revenge is coming and this is how it starts...

I was part of the standby crew selected to fly to Andrews Airbase in Washington at 2pm on 9/11. We flew down the Eastern seaboard where I was able to see the massive disaster that had happened in real time from 25000 ft. I will never forget the smoke: it was like an island in the sky. I wrote the poem in the Holiday Inn where I stayed overnight awaiting the return flight to the UK.

The flight home was so surreal as radio silence remained all the way through and no vapour trails in the air. Felt like apocalypse; probably was...

On returning to the UK I was promoted and moved to yet another job, this time at Chequers (the weekend residence of the Prime Minister). I held the post of Deputy House Manager, a job I loved. However, as everything in my life isn't easy, it wasn't long before I was moving on again...

House of Ghosts

In the English Countryside is a grand house of ghosts.
Over the years has had a number of hosts.
Each one has a different idea,
Each one will bend the rules and not adhere;
Some stay a long time and make great change,
Some stay a short time and are quite strange.
Decisions are made, good and bad,
Some of which can make lives sad.
Dinner parties and entertaining and frivolity
Whilst people are fighting for the country.
The rooms of Chequers are draped in pain
From past dignitaries imprisoned and shamed;
From great leaders with drinking ways,
From amazing travellers whose treasure decays.
Chequers provides a mighty hiding place
Where world leaders meet face to face.
Great announcement are made to the nation,
Some of which destroy life's creation:
Decisions to start wars and invade,
And a place where certain prime ministers stopped and
    prayed.
A room from where condolence letters were written
By an Iron Lady who loved Great Britain.
She wrote to the family of every taken soul
To try and help with their now black hole,
A hole there was no explanation for.
The dear men lost in the Falklands War
Invade Iraq, without a care,
Another decision that was made by a man who did care.
Signing the death warrant to soldiers great
Is not an easy decision to make.
Chequers is used for rest and relaxation,
Within this job you can't hide from aggravation.
Ghosts will always roam the corridors' grounds
Until one day true peace can be found...

Tony Blair, who was Prime Minister at this time, visited Chequers with his lovely family most weekends. Even though Chequers is a retreat, Mr Blair worked constantly, as did his wife. I wrote the poem after a press conference whilst the house was being closed up ready for the next visit.

After the relative calm of my life so far (!) the following years taught me the extremes of war – all recorded in poetry in the section that follows. Anger, misery, pain and truth were my inspiration and frustration was my pen.

WAR

In the Shadows

In the shadows they hide
Protecting themselves from the hurt inside.

In the shadows they lay
Hoping for a future, for a brighter day.

In the shadows they dwell
Shielding themselves from the outside hell.

In the shadows they linger
Waiting for the world to point the finger.

In the shadows they remain
Hiding from cruelty, hate and disdain.

In the shadows they cower
Under bombardment from a superpower.

In the shadows they poise
Fingers in ears stopping the noise.

From the shadows they will come
Frightened, fearful, damaged and numb.

Into the light that they long for,
To colour and happiness and things they adore.

The shadow is now killed by the light,
But it won't be gone long; it will soon be night.

A Thought, a Dream

A thought, a dream
Of life and how it seems:
Watching children playing in the dirt,
Surrounded by pain and hurt.
Still with happiness in their eyes,
When missiles litter the skies
Turning dirt into blood,
Demolishing buildings, tearing up the cud.
Still the children smile and play.
War continues every day,
While the smiles remain,
All morals and principles are flushed down the drain.
Men fight to save their land,
Only to destroy what was made by nature's hand.
Still death becomes the normality
With disfigurement and heartache for all the world to see.
A thought, a dream turns into a nightmare
For all those to see and none to care.

Fancy a Cuppa

"Fancy a cup of tea?" he said,
Even though around us laid the dead.

"Two sugars in yours and black?" he said,
Still the bodies lay motionless and dead.

"Won't be long before the kettle is boiled,"
Still the bodies lay on the floor dirty and soiled.

"Pass me your cup, it will be ready in a while,"
The smell of death lays heavy and vile.

"Oh lovely," he said, "just how Mum makes!"
The pools of blood are flowing now into lakes.

A slurp a guzzle and then it's gone,
Just like the deads' lights, they are no longer on.

Better be on our way and get back to base,
Stepping over bodies that now have no face.

Don't drink tea anymore,
Chills me inside and rips up my core.
Prefer coffee now...

Afghan Colours

Colours in the sky
Like radiant fabric dye,
Sun piercing through the sky is dark red,
With black darkened clouds like large lumps of lead.
Clay and sand colours litter the ground
With piercing blue streaks like darts surround.
White plumes of grey tint fluffy clouds
In golden sun glinting they cover like shrouds.
Orange mud buildings silhouetted against the sky
Splashes of colour on the buildings like tie-dye.
The sparkle and glint of fresh metallic,
The absorption of the deep colour of faded plastic:
Colours reflecting happiness and light,
Some still visible in the starkness of bright light.
Darkness in the desert brings dark shades of blue,
Black and the final glint of orange shines through.
No artificial glows of light anywhere,
The colour of darkness in the desert is rare.

Hotel Built for Fun

The constant firing
Exposed all the wiring
Of the hotel used for fun.

A dictator's retreat
Where evil can meet
Is why this war had begun.

People ejected
The building is neglected
And the government is overun.

The dictator is replaced
Its contents displaced
And another war is done.

All that remains is anger and pain,
Money-making builders with a crane.

As a nation rebuilds
And its occupants are healed.

Awaiting the failure
Of another dictator,

And the cycle to return
And the new builds burn.

While society decides
Which leader will reside
In the hotel built for fun.

Heated Fear

It's so hot the sun is burning.
I'm so scared my stomach's churning.
It's so noisy my ears are aching.
I'm so scared my body is shaking.
It's so bright my eyes are a-squint.
I'm so anxious my heart's on the brink.
I'm so tired my body aches.
It's so intense the earth it quakes.
I'm so confused my mind is a mess.
I'm quivering all over with the stress.
It's so nauseating this putrid smell.
I'm thinking nice thoughts to remove me from hell.
It's so frustrating this terrible war.
I'm praying for and end or a truce to draw.
It's so annoying talks and negotiations never work.
I'm fed up of human rights getting the shirk.
It's just as I expected from the human race.
Going round in circles in total disgrace.

A Grey Colourful Day

The colour of sand
Isn't normally brown:
It can be golden with glitter when you look down.
The Afghanistan sand here is grey
Mirroring the boring repetitive days.
Sometimes it's red with a bit of burnt umber,
Impelling dreams of hope, beauty and wonder.
When it is red here, someone has died,
And there are dark circles where others have cried.
Sometimes it's yellow with speckles of black;
Its black here from a missile attack.
Sometimes it's like pink pieces of coral.
Its oil-stained here, tainted by people with no morals.
It can be multi-coloured where children have played,
It can be petrol-stained where a petrol tank has laid.
It can have green flecks and clear crystals:
Shrapnel from attacks of air-to-ground missiles.
Sometimes the sand looks black and white,
And it glistens and glows in the darkness of night.
Always the desert sands hide secrets in their colour
And the Afghan desert has a history like no other.

'Take cover...'

Take cover, there is a missile,
Which happened once in a while:
A beautiful engineered streak of white
Which destructive force came both day and night.
Weapon of such cowardly force
Causing pain and anger in due course.

Careful, there is a mine:
A small piece of metal in the sand did shine,
Hidden like a shiny gem in the ground.
It will reach up and bite you without a sound.
Then to disappear without a trace,
A sly weapon without a face,
Remaining dormant for years to come,
Hiding, waiting for the stray foot to drum.

Quick, hide, there is a drone,
On the horizon, gathering intelligence alone.
Taking pictures, sneaking around,
Giving off a slight buzzing sound.
No threat, you say, just pictures taken,
But with this information you are mistaken,
For its devious manner is a destructive force:
Killing and maiming is par for the course,
Feeding the missiles and bombs that are dropped,
A Dark photographer that cannot be stopped.

Watch out, there is a man:
The most evil weapon they cannot ban,
Deceptive and repulsive, they will kill on sight.
This evil weapon's bark is as bad as its bite.
There is no cure, no way it can stop,
Until civilisation has gone to pop.
They can be restrained, distracted and stalled,
But the end result death will be called.

You Don't Know Me

You don't know me,
Why do you hate me?
Why are we fighting?
Your anger is frightening:
Why are we angry?
You say you want to be free.
I won't stop you, it's not my fault.
We got stuck in a war and I got caught.
I want you to be happy and have some fun.
I don't want to die and this be over life done.
Can't we be friends, talk a little and laugh?
Or at least agree and chat? Small steps in halves.
We can put it right, sort out the problem,
All live together and not condemn.
We can do it, you don't need to be educated;
Killing and evil are so overrated.
We could live apart and not even talk,
Meet up occasionally and go for a walk,
Or we can listen to what the powers will say:
Kill each other and not see another day.
Living is far better than the alternative.
We could even be friends, talk and give.
What are we talking about? Who cares, anyway?
Lets walk away from each other and fight another day.

Cross the Border

We have been given the order
To cross the border,
To play with our fate
And liberate
A team forever.
Fighting together,
Full of pride and strength,
We cut through the fence
To make our presence known
In the moonscape place the enemy calls home.
Driving in, we meet no resistance,
Pushing on to solidify our existence.
The enemy is running,
The British are coming:
Running with terror in their eyes,
As we push on with our allies,
Standing forever tall,
Not stopping until Baghdad falls.
Bombarding with fire and pain,
Killing without even a hint of shame,
Ripping families lives apart,
Pictures of sadistic war art:
All these things stamped in our memory,
Returning as the evil PTSD.
Never shall or would we forget
The little resistance that was met
To kill and remove a sadistic dictator:
Where his statue stood is now a crater.
Sadness in people's eyes will remain
Until they find another dictator to blame.

'It's Christmas here'

It's Christmas here:
There is no cheer,
No decorations or balloons,
No laughing or festive tunes,
No sleeping in a big chair;
Just loneliness, because nobody cares.
No presents to unwrap or games to play,
Just wishes that would end the day.
No happiness and joy,
No family to annoy,
Just a tent, a bed and a book,
And a mess tent with a terrible Christmas dinner cooked.
Lots of people trying to smile and grin,
Blocking out the desert mess were in.
Not just a bad Christmas for me:
Outside the wire things are terrible, you can see.
Children in rags, dirty and not fed;
Men with clothes showing where they bled.
War is always a two-sided affair,
With one side worse off and the other side to care.
This war will never really end,
We will leave and aid parcels they will send.
Nothing will really change,
People will swap lives and governments will rearrange.
Still the hate will exist
And the anger and blame for them will persist.
But it's Christmas here, pull a cracker and pretend
All is good and dreams haven't come to an end.

Watch and Shoot

On a cold desert night when the air is still
A motionless sniper takes aim to kill.
Shepherds tending their sheep
Soon will be hiding, cowering and meek.
Bullets will exchange to show who's boss,
And the losing side will incur that loss.
Still the hiding and waiting game remains,
Shooting and killing the beast will tame.
A sniper, though, has only one thought:
To take the shot and not get caught.
It seems the coward's way to fight,
No challenges or speech just a flash in the night.
Perhaps this is the best way
As speech and negotiation are a waste of the day.
It's a quick decision to press and run
No thoughts as to why or who has been stung.
But in wars there are no rules,
Just a big man waving his painful tools.
To reap destruction, hate and pain
Until there is no life and quietness doth remain.

Under Attack

Still dense smoke-filled air,
A bright red light from a flare,
Noise distant and near,
Voices crackling with anger and fear.
Orders are barked and directions are given,
Confusion occurs and panic within.
More noise, flashes and the smell of fire,
Anxiety levels and fear mounts higher and higher.
More bangs and shouting still rain down,
For men who signed to defend her crown.
Running in all directions, finding a safe place,
Brothers in arms, all colours, creed and race.
Together they assemble as a mighty troop,
Rescuing the injured, keeping strong the group.
Together they stand, together they fall,
With no thought of themselves or selfishness at all.
Until all men are safe and away from harm
And peacefulness resumes, restoring calm.
After the attack comes the response:
A team of angry men working, revenge they want.
And so the cycle repeats again:
Its not how will they die, it's going to be when.

Medical Evacuation

In the dead of night
On a homeward flight,
Another unfortunate man
Heading to hospital in Birmingham:
A casualty of war
On a Middle Eastern tour.
Patients with tubes and a medical team
Show you what war really does mean:
Death, destruction and physical harm,
Missing limbs, a leg and an arm,
And the hidden injury of PTSD,
Causing men to hide worry and flee.
The torture of war will continue to grow
And its hidden pain in anger it will show.
Charities will help with money and care
But what the soldier needs is someone to be there,
Someone to talk to listen and believe,
To take away hurt and let them grieve
For the loss of brothers and their enlisted kin,
Knowing they were fighting the war we would never win.

Missile Deception

Another missile rips a family in two,
Five more are launched and death will ensue.
Rains of destructive bouncing balls,
The black cloud of lifeless destruction falls,
Cloaking the ground in a sea of blood,
Burying the bodies in the stench of the mud.
Crying and heartache echoes in the air,
More missiles are launched without a care.
Life has no meaning anymore,
The sight of death is knocking on their door.
Every family will know somebody who died,
And the pilgrims will have the pain of death inside.
Nomadic their existence,
Strong their persistence,
But still the grasp of death will follow,
Cutting through their bodies disease will hollow,
Until there is no more crying in the air.
The fortunate will view on television without a care.
Death is the victims' only release
As they lay on the bodies of the relatives beneath.
A lottery of life is their only game
These people will die without a name.
Carnage and death is all they saw;
To the Western world, it's just another war.

Vilification Negative

For a man to get vilified
Usually means someone has died.
Within war lots of people are killed
Even civilians' lives won't be fulfilled.
Death, destruction and lives ripped apart,
Flattened cities are only the start.
People cannot begin again from that.
Out of the rebuild, large company cats get fat.
But nobody remembers the men that died,
Only the person who gets vilified.
Seems strange how one person can take the blame
Whilst the world around them is going insane.
It's true the soldier he has no rights,
Just the instruction to stand and fight.
If he questions or asks for a reason,
The law states that's nothing but treason.
So just the man who gets vilified,
He takes the blame which rips up his insides.
For he is the one who killed and maimed,
And why the soldier's grave is unnamed.
He is the one that should be vilified
Out of respect for the people who obeyed and died,
For the ones who dared to advise
They will carry the guilt to their death inside.

My time in the military may now have finished, with wars long since gone. For me, though, the wars still continue; but these ones are the most sinister of all – the wars of the mind.